SHIPPEN

Dawn Bauling

Indigo Dreams Publishing

First Edition: Shippen
First published in Great Britain in 2014 by:
Indigo Dreams Publishing
24, Forest Houses
Cookworthy Moor
Halwill
Beaworthy
Devon
EX21 5UU

www.indigodreams.co.uk

Dawn Bauling has asserted her right under the Copyright, Designs and Patents Act 1988 to be identified as the author of this work.
© 2014 Dawn Bauling

ISBN 978-1-909357-04-4

British Library Cataloguing in Publication Data. A CIP record for this book can be obtained from the British Library.

Designed and typeset in Palatino Linotype by Indigo Dreams.

Cover design by Ronnie Goodyer at Indigo Dreams.
Section images by Ronnie Goodyer at Indigo Dreams
Printed and bound in Great Britain by Imprint Academic, Exeter.

To Ronnie, who reads my skies at night
and merries my paths by day.

Acknowledgements

Thanks must go to our friends Ruth and Chris Boswell who allowed us the use of their Shippen for many years and Geoff and Lorraine who helped us find our own in North Devon. We loved your houses before we loved our own. Thanks to Deborah Harvey for allowing me to use a line from her beautiful book, Dart, and to Les and Angie who have shown me even more of the beauty of the south west. And finally to Linus and Valerie whose gentle encouragements, unknown to them, kept me focussed on finishing this collection when events conspired against it.

Many of these poems have featured in Reach Poetry and one or two in Poetry Cornwall.

i.m June Rita Steward

Previous Publications

Loud Voices In The Quiet Child, IDP, 2008

❧ CONTENTS ❧

Shippen 11

❧ FIELD

Stick gathering at Golitha Falls 15
Helping me to breathe 16
Sunday Morning With Vaughan 18
Kiss Me Quick 20
Finding The Quiet In Stone 21
Round Up 22
Black Fox 23
Cornish Border 24
Rock Sand 25
Waiting At St. Enedoc's 26
Dry Stick 27
Scree Running 28
Mother River 29
River 30
Rapids 31

❧ GATE

Reveille 35
Mist 36
Morning Coffee Tasting 37
On days like this 38
Night Wind 39
A Small Exhibition 40
Fence 41

Cafe On The Green 41

Song in A 42

Map Folding For Beginners 43

Weather Break 44

The Olive Branch Café 45

Winter cupped 46

haiku 47

❦ HEARTH

Light Thought 51

Old Sowtontown 52

Holiday Snap 53

Trenannick 54

Held 55

A Consultation of Nails 56

Rings 57

Stones 58

And so the clock ticks 59

Swallowing My Father 60

Truth Stone 61

Harmony 62

As Laura Speaks 63

And All Other People 64

❦ LOFT

These Unexpected Schoolgirl Fancies 67

Love-in-Idleness 68

Night Thought 69

Stolford 69

Dust 70

Hand Words 71

Swan 72

River Exe mussels with chilli, tomato and parsley 73

Over the Table 74

A Late Bloom 75

Henna On Her hands 76

Sentence.. 78

Shall I Write 79

Given 80

SHIPPEN

"...she who'd been wont to dust even the shippen!"
Deborah Harvey, Dart

Shippen

I will take the platinum pins
from my silent sea of silver hair,
let its spirals tumble down
to the briar and bracken.

He will know my shadow.

I will unbutton crystal on a last coat,
show him the skin he patterned
in paths, pearled with aconite
and tobacco kisses like jewels.

He will unpick my patchwork.

I will unlace stifled boots,
uncurl my toes from their tight bindings
to a dance of truth and freedoms
beyond the light canopy.

He will hold me if I fall.

Then I will tip back my head
and howl across threads of moonlight
delivered on a slim canvas of night
as a long, slow deliverance.

It is an animal releasing.
The land will sing
through the tremble of a day
as it welcomes the voice of a soul
in the shippen.

Field

Stick gathering at Golitha Falls

If every stick or stone
in my bag and boot
on this unexceptional day
had a walk attached
all valley tied, fell studded
plain or plimsoll,
even barefoot tired ,
I would have enough.
They would be my wood,
my hedge and beach,
my cottage hearth beside,
each one turned
and seasoned by a hand,
a paw, a storm,
a child or tide;
a better gathering tied
under the chiselled hazel
lintel of my heart
unbriared.

Helping me to breathe

We took the running dog
through the fields up to the long wood,
quiet at first, and careful
with each other in the wet.
You showed me your tracks,
the favourite places,
so I would have them later
and breathed woodbreath
through my hair, close to my lips
enough for me to taste you.

Mud covered, I noticed
how your face shone even in cloud light,
younger with dog years,
glossed, like a favourite coat.
You asked for a kiss I had been
waiting for too many lives to give,
laughing as rain fell sideways
down our necks in rivers
ready for us to follow.

Hand fasted, you had the words
I had been pressing in linen
all ready in your mouth
interlacing me with their wood echoes.
You touched in white wind and ink
soaking my tight bindings
until I was stained with letters
wet on wet, skin milk,
drowning in your meaning
cut with scent.

And so you led me waterwards
gentle in path and briarbound
to hear mother river calling
my name, my real name in her depth.
Teach me her secrets in sticks
in pebble and bedrock,
in bankside and flood.
Let me flow naked
forgetting the coat I must put on
when the current breaks.
Whisper the words of a homecoming
to help me to breathe.

Sunday Morning With Vaughan

(a response to Lark Ascending)

Bold on this high sky
I have been granted wings
by an Englishman.

With small notes
his hands have sewn bright feathers
on to a woman's wilting skin

given flight from within
intangible to tangible
in the openness of thermals.

I'll soar to the north's
rock walls and waters,
to rough raw-edged fell tops,

dip deep in the drowning lakes
to moor and mountain,
to small-handled cottage door.

I'll coast lazy to the south
riding the diamond sea storms,
diving in salt wind crags

past boat and basking crab men
shark sharp rock
to fast scatter children.

I'll slide centreways, gentle
to my beloved river man, our dog
stood in a dark bogwood waiting.

Then circle, rest, his lark
a note that plucks a new life
and gives height to heavy nothing;

my birdbreath beating
bone deep music delivered
through his soft fingers

to my hallows
as the window cracks.
See. I have landed. At last

unjessed.

Kiss Me Quick

I shall never wear a hat
with Kiss Me Quick upon it.
The notion has no merit.
Not even with rock
and candyfloss sitting on my lips
did I want a kiss to be quick,
surprising some puppy boy.
Slow, yes and ponderous –
a thinker's kiss that learns cleverly
samples delicately aware
of environment and shade.
Quick has no future or promise;
slow has a right to roam, to hold
without rush or the squealing
brakes of a getaway car.
There must be time to taste
each subtle spice, separate, divine,
not pecked in single bite.
This kiss I am offering
will not consider brevity.
It is slow as oak and fine
as orchid, as an open road and
more beautiful than a benediction.
So come to me at every gate
and let me show you;
never kiss me quick.

Finding The Quiet In Stone
(sitting in Wistman's Wood)

So, this is the place
we chose to sit,
lit in cinder
chipped with granite.

Its greens come harder
litmus from beneath
bleached
with sour light.

The stone rolls
its mossed skin,
making silver blisters
for its pain.

Mouths are pebbled,
rock-tongued,
unworded. Thought
hangs in beards.

No new-age here
only old priests
and our fallen altars –
pure bleak retreat.

Come not for laughter
in this better air.
Ask the gods for old arts
to bring the land

peace.

Round Up

Because the pack is separated
he worries between us
trying to tidy us
into one place.

He cares too much,
doesn't understand
such independent ways,
his grey brows fretting,
squeaking at our recalcitrance,
points racing back and forth.

It is an impossible round up.

Later, sure
that the door is closed
and we are roomed,
settee'd and full of tea,
he will sleep like a newborn,
all care gone, complete.

We envy the ease
of collies.

Black Fox

Our own black fox
hunts the downs
quicker than a spectre,
feet sharp, like arrow heads
finding a course.
He merries our path,
pink-bounced, ripped sticked
unclipped to freedom.
He has backward eyes
laser-light, sloe-black
bullets that miss nothing,
steeling the ewes
nervous in audience
now robbed of an easy sun.
They do not want his hurry,
the snap and round coarse
to sheep hippyness.
He will take his pleasure
in minutes, defying hours.

Our own black fox
hunts the downs
giving the day a path.
The dog allows
the man.

Cornish Border

On the border he inflates,
fluffs out a little as if
only now his feathers fit.

Buzzard man, he will walk a little taller,
nearer the sky on the up draft
brace-backed and plump-skinned.

His stride is longer
the muscle suddenly fed rich
and pheasant proud,

his eyes less filled
with unknown restless melancholy
luminescent and tendered.

And so my female swells and struts
content, compelled to seed
soon seasons to be our ordinary,

raftered, treed or cob-walled close
know but not flown from yet
grown Cornish.

Rock Sand

Out over the bar
where the tide has left its beads
a woman garners sticks
and pockets pebbles, listening
to the language of shells;
a son learns how
to fly a kite
swallowing small disappointments
for one proud flight;
a widow takes a lung full
of wide-aired comfort,
forward again for the first time;
by the steps a mother pushes a pram
determined to pluck pleasure
from stolen hours, child-glad
and happy with her sea drug;
yachts have been laid sideways,
abandoned, owners anchored now
by a ball and dog;
lucky travellers are ferry-plucked
and zigzagged over
to the harbour-of-slow-speeds,
obedient at last;
the walkers yomp,
grandparents wander,
the child yells as
the poet writes –
all able to afford
the sand at Rock .

Waiting At St. Enedoc's

He swells
like a tide
sat next to John
at St Enedoc's.

He is puffed
like a pipe,
ripened
like a pippin.

The bells of the Immacolata
called him long ago
before words were on a page
and we had found him.

And this, his wish
beyond a bag full of sand
salvages and steers
daylight through my bar.

He is here
in the links, daffodilled,
dune and thistles
in his turn-ups
He is here.
The father and the son.
The poet and
the pilgrim.

Dry Stick

Under each dry stick
a bud may form
if the quick scald of fire
releases it.

You thought I had no life
within. Such foolery.
I was a red fire lily
dancing on a bright wind
who would leave
pollen on your trousers,
for the want of a match.

Scree Running

Prehistoric
sharp-sided spits
of rock litter
our path
like dropped hurts
that if fallen upon
will pierce or wound.
Unafraid now
of where they will move
I kick out
trampling each inconvenience
like old weight
clinging to my boots
until all are sand
enough to take my feet
to the sea.

Mother River

Your water
belly accepts this poor pilgrim
like a mother welcoming
a first child.

She stands in your deep flow
with empty hands.
Ice knives renew the amniotic
for her rebirth.

Naked in the pure drowning,
she accepts the tides rip,
a life's exfoliation.
as her beginning.

The brooding water
delivers its new child, naiad
in a baptism of river tunes
to silver Tethys.

Opening the buttons
of your wet blouse
mother river suckles
with weed embroidered breasts.

Blushed girl sudden pure
woman rushes to the fringes
of your bank, cocoon free and
easy with anointing

finally –
her first real day.

River

Speighted and pleased
to be running free
not clear and bird-gentle
but mudded
native, like a teenager
on a skateboard doing loops
and dodges all the way down
to the sea yelling
untamed obscenities.

Rapids

The river rolls
rapids over
stone cold fingers

Gate

Reveille

A woodpecker shoots up the morning –
guerrilla, fast-gattling to his troops.

Three eager sparrows, intent on bush deployment
inspect their combats, beaks boot-shiny.

A pigeon muezzins smooth minims through a cooled chimney
amplified, pregnant with undernotes; kind bugler.

A pheasant gobbles the morning's rations
skiffling its chores in advance of gun and road.

A chiff-chaff laughs at clumsy land manoeuvres
dimpling the day with its light left-right air boots.

I tell myself, under my net of stone,
that I have left wild ravens behind.

You, who prophesied with phoenix feathers,
were right. After one night's fire

you said that the birds would wake me.

Mist

The hill's opal mist
opens our morning window –
gifts of ancient gems
where your eyes have been.

Morning Coffee Tasting

Unsure of your taste
I have sent you coffee
Monsoon Malabar and Black Java
with names to dance treacled
love notes on your tongue.

Spoon them gently, measuring
each cascade, their rich aroma
a cadence.
Inhale the dark incense,
filling the spaces of your room
like a new woman
turning the first light to
perfume in the air as you drink.

Ask me to join you one day
beyond the pulse of this thought;
ask me to share your cup
while it runs over.

On days like this

On days like this
you may not see
but there are scales forming
below my breasts
and my back itches
for want of a fin.
The two foolish feet
unreliable with year
are pulling together
wanting to be welded
tailed silently
as slippery rudders.
My ears are filled
with eddy and silt
underneath echoes
loud tongued
yet languageless
to swim, to pull
to rise up.

I have been given
a waterfall as a gift
below my bedroom window.
I am the fish that leaps
that glistens for you
within it.

Night Wind

Night wind is dancing with the door
too loose in its frame with want.
I shall not mind its late rhythms
for it has served me well and let
your lost voice through.

Night light is dancing on the walls
too tight with habit to let me out.
I shall not mind the shadows though
for they hold strangers in their hands
to give darkness a new truth.

Night songs are playing with my heart
too delicate from battle to lie.
I shall embrace these part people as I can
for they are listening companions,
lovers for my solitude.

And when I am free to open the door,
and break blind walls
and carry my heart whole,
I shall not need to speak in riddles
nor wait for the night to pattern them to you.

A Small Exhibition

Talking of portraits
and me in the wrong glasses
looking for lines and focus,
saying I preferred blurred edges
and curves, lieing,
and about the rain.

And her asking for clarity
not ambiguity, gouache
over pastel and sharp
photos to work from
like on her exquisite mobile,
mine hidden, not able
to barter numbers or frame.

And you waiting outside holding
the lead, wondering
what was taking so long,
almost patient and damp
from today and yesterday's crags,
still smiling.

A small exhibition.
Two women talking of art,
the weather and dogs
wondering

what more is there.

Fence

Bradgate's red framework
Robin on a barbed-wire fence
Autumn surprises

Cafe On The Green

Hot
Tea
Pleasures
Sticky jammed
Buttery-fingered
Widecombe Thursday leaves its mark.

Song in A

Hinckley Point sings its low bass
in A over the mud flat

over the flood plane
where the rough-edged cottages
get harder under their salt shells

over the skeleton reeds
of Steart Point and all its dark
suspicions

over Dunster's pastel cobbles,
its floral knicknackery,
over its low-fat fudge

over the flint-coated horses
trying to oblige and find
only this year's grass

over the well-pressed trousers of
the solitary man
and his singular view.

We tut at its Russian angles,
angry at such charcoal bluntness
next to our hills and postcard seas,
air-brushing its austerity
whilst we make ourselves
another cup of tea
with a kettle that trills
in high C.

Map Folding For Beginners

Each time we fold the map
its joins become a little loose –
only slightly at first,
imperceptible, like a leak.
Small parish boundaries blur
contours go missing,
a forest lost.
But with each new turn,
each volte-face
and reinvention or requirement of a route,
roads and rivers
houses and hills
disappear within the crease
until one day
without realising what you had done
the whole thing falls apart
and you wished
you had left everything alone,
had no desire to travel
and stayed exactly where you were,
where you were really meant to be.

Weather Break

The clouds are within me
storming, twisting from the west
in birth throes
troubling what lies within.

The trees are here,
rustling their shushing rhythms
like flamenco dancers
in blood red dresses.

The rain pours through me
spilling tears down the window
pain in this sobbing room
battering like bullets.

The wind is in me
stirring buried desire
from its shallow grave
in a cascade of gypsy girl hair.

Thunder and lightning safe
in skin's tight sealed casket
are heaving quietly in small explosions
earthshaking –

the night is here
caught in a dark velvet dress
and bare feet wet with stars
from their long walking.

As I catch your eye
will you still call me child?

The Olive Branch Café

Convivial with coffee froth, we allow *The Olive Branch* to spread its butter knife and walnut bonhomie even as we stand in a ramshackle queue for the toilet. We pretend our bladders are still fully obedient to our minds and effect purpose by reading the plaque about Prince Rupert and Bill Bryson who had both paid a visit here – men who probably wouldn't have had to wait. We are envious of their male efficiency and the disc that reads 'vacant' on their door.

Drama trained, we greet the eccentric lady in the pink wig and green felt hat like a sister as she emerges many minutes later, her pockets bulging with toilet rolls. We think we are not like her – relieved. We are more polished, fresh with history and pompous with new-met sisters. We know we will disown each other as soon as the door closes, as the queue advances.

We tell our befriended strangers that *'We* won't take long', superior with control, comradely recognition of each others' urgency; a precious feminine intimacy. We know we will be good users of tissue. Such things matter.

On the way back to old friends, we take the wrong staircase and end up in the staff kitchen, pretending we had always meant to take this route, adjusting our felt hat by way of apology. The witnesses smile.

Contrition comes easy. It's the rest that is hard.

Winter cupped

Not a dark cup this year
not cloudy fluid
with the potential to scald
or choke in the chest

A fine glass for toasting
brighter than orange
with russets on the tongue
long-lasting, warm-hearted

A filled grail, wild wooded
leaf-light, overflowing with fox
and bubbles up the nose
giggles down the throat

A whole known goblet
for holding high on this paper morning
we kings and queens
of forest and sea

Loving you, though lost;
licking this first Christmas
free.

haiku

Thin drips of light lace
rattle leaf bells ice clappered
wood peels its winter

Hearth

Light Thought

I sleep like a dog
between walks
stirring only for food.

I lie with my legs apart
bearing too much flesh
like a harlot

sitting outside cheese shops,
drooling at fat
men passing with pasties.

I snore like a bishop
in sun, open-mouthed,
plumply, pompously operatic.

I run into water
ready to be swallowed,
shaking a torrent of hair

at tourists careful
with coats, carrot sticks
and peevish low-cal rock.

My breasts hang free,
my zip's undone,
my laughter peels bar-maid
brassy and beer-bright

bubbling at last,

I am sybarite, I am epicure,
I am a woman on holiday.

Old Sowtontown
before the curtains are pulled

There are pre-Raphaelite skies
over Brentor,
clouds awaiting their gods,
the older masters to arrive.
The paint is still wet
in the late light
bronze, sifted with inconsistent
blue and mauve.
Our fingers work
tracing an outline
through smeared glass
attempting to shape this day
to trumpet it
with pure notes
like poets.
Our breath mists the view
as we hold up a loose sun
with thought,
the glass cold
against hot ambition.

Holiday Snap

(for Heather)

Heather
flat on a ply board
in a loose school costume
proficiency badges plumping
her new bosom.
She is one long match
in a battled white-hinged swim-hat,
her rubber crown for stayfast curls.
She torpedoes the waves
with whoops,
brown hair cooped
looped and harboured
safe for another mother supper time.

And me
in red bubble shorts
nipple-bare baiting the sea's edge,
a boygirl in a push of surf
with nevermind white hair
and sand in my crotch,
wanting to be six years older;
wanting her to teach me
how to do that too.

Trenannick

Today I know I am rich.
I have pasty, beer and fresh
love on my breath.
I have a purse with a few unspent pounds,
a full fridge
and four new books by the bedside.
My clothes are clean,
(apart from a few pasty crumbs)
my hair full of cliff wind,
my feet warm and their toes painted.
My ears are overweight
with the laughter of birds:
a cacophony of sparrows carousing
by a window where chickens meander
like women at boot sales.
The dog is asleep in front of
his non-conformist log-burner.
I have an orange in my pocket
and forgotten what a watch is for.
I have lost all useful telephone numbers.
I will whisper *I love you*
to a man, just after I have read him this
with words I have discovered
leaning on the arm of a chair.
Knowing, he will smile.

We are in Cornwall.
Today I know I am rich.

Held

She will not allow me
freedom to leave
the high banks this year.

She frowns through white cottages,
twists the lines in The Strand,
at The Point when the road bends north

and I hear her growing pains
in a pheasant shout, a gull cry
with the sea wind's sharp slap.

I cannot fool the forest path
or the cottage hearth
with two week happiness.

There must be more.

She knows.
If I cannot be born
I must be adopted.

In this mean time
she asks me to pay my dues,
so I leave her the pulse

of a heart for her to find,
like a girl after eggs
hidden in a tree hole
at the end of a Cornish drive.

A Consultation of Nails
To H. F.

She had beautiful nails –
green like pines
white-tipped with snow,
with aconites.

She said she could do better,
was just lending her nails
for others to learn on,
the brushwork imperfect.

She could make small worlds
on the nails she painted
from the calmness of her soul.
She had a trade of marvels.

I wanted her to take mine,
my beetle nails and torn moons,
and mix me a palette;
her unique universe,

so, whilst she rubbed ridges
and polished me smooth,
placing constellations in the darkness
and easing me,

I could tell her carefully
of the nature of bruises,
of how things fade
and even crushed fingers can become beautiful.

They have the strength to open
any world they choose.

Rings

Because the gold has worn
thin on my finger
and the ring grown loose
I will take gabbro and serpentine
and forge myself another
as a promise,
silver this time,
firm as rock.

Stones
(at Blackingstone Rock)

Where you are round
I am flat;
your song
my whistle;
weathered smoothness
to dull my bristle
and angles that are
made suddenly curves.

We are at times
unalike
as leaf and flame

but together
inexplicably
logan stones
balanced perfectly
forever.

And so the clock ticks

Now the door has closed
and the whirlwind of others gone,
we sit in the new stilled sunlight
stretching toes like cats.

Today the dust motes have settled,
whilst noise sleeps relaxed, at home,
humming occasionally for comfort,
like an unserviced boiler.

We are not so young we have to touch,
not too familiar to have forgotten why
it is necessary, accepting the promise of slow
so something otherwise can treat us.

We hold our Sunday rhythm close
in the risk of each other's heartbeat,
knowing the gift of this time is
as beautiful as listening to an old clock tick.

Swallowing My Father

When they examine my mother
they will discover small parts of my father
hiding like stowaways inside her:

his muscles keeping her upright ,
good bones to improve her stoop,
joints to stop hers crumbling,
a rare glint, a defiance of chin.

When he knew he was disappearing
he had told her to nibble in
just what she would need,
spilling himself into her

until she could hold his shape,
and walk upright,
until he was emptied out
and able to go.

Raising her glass to him daily
she will confess with such love
it had always been this way.

Truth Stone

(to my children at Christmas)

Even if I had not
given you a portion
of your life

Even if you did not
hear the sigh of the world
as you each first breathed

Even if you had been
made adult
as you are now
and knowing –

I believe
some gentle god
would have brought you
to me anyway
like a seed on air
or a star
so I could watch you live
and navigate.

Even though I am not
shepherd-wise
this thing I know –

It is my truth stone.

Harmony

I ask you to listen
sitting under the evening lamp.
Your ears are trained to such things –
the delicate nuances of music.
You carry melody
on a careful palm
like prophesies spoke over you;
words on a boyskin.

Though you do not recognise
the tune I now offer,
you will seek its clever beat,
the tumble easy in your head.
Your hands find the deep
notes to transform.
Your cheeks are heralds.

Lost in a crescendo,
I watch you understand
what I am sending
in our ragged arrangement.
Jarring and soaring,
I will try to find a place to land.

Beyond the music
we will find a song
Beyond the singing
harmony.

As Laura Speaks

(for Chris on his wedding day)

You will not have known
the day I sat
beneath the crab-apple tree
until evening.

You were in a turtle suit
or cape, with a sword down your back;
in Lincoln green with tights and
a feather on your hat.
It was sometime after your front teeth
but before a girl's kiss.

You didn't know
I was dreaming large
dreams as big
as a holiday with speedboats
to last a lifetime.

You couldn't know
I was summoning
your half, your split-apart
the one you would be closer to than skin.

You were too young,
too mettlesome.

But I will tell you now,
my pip, my little other,
so you will see those dreams too.

They will open on your face
as Laura speaks

and they will last a lifetime.

And All Other People

(listening to *You and Me* by Lifehouse)

I thought I had become hard,
a stone on a beach
rubbed until only the granite
heart was visible with a few lines
of serpentine where light
had rested from the ancient.

But when I saw you spin
her, hair blown by your breath
her eyes the fulcrum,
your feet conjoined, cogged,

I found I was pressed clay
in your dancers hands,
one of your other people,
a ripple unnoticed
in the dark parts of a room
being transformed.

Loft

These Unexpected Schoolgirl Fancies

These unexpected schoolgirl fancies
have tied knots round the rough surface
of her disappointment rubbing it
smooth like a wet stone.

They have laid dewlight and feathersilk
on a withering twig until it is transfigured,
blushed bright, green-tipped and budded
open-legged in a low afternoon.

Inconsummate they will dance
like spun sycamore keys, two-podded
yet together, heady lovers twisting
in the world's waltz, unmindful of settling.

In her mind she can be all things
under the possibility of a gaze.

Love-in-Idleness

Close on a night that sticks
I dally with a witches craft,
casting you.

Naked I make two-handed
Ouijas across the cello
of your back

bowing over your waist
and plucking forests
by scroll and peg shedding dust.

Hecate plays pure tonight,
her crows muffled, newt-eyes damned
her incantations silent as a cure.

I still you by signs, run
runes and glyphs by finger tip.
It is a Sylkie's work.

Only as the poison is lip-sealed
do you stir. No deadly night's shade
just heart's ease.

       (*Love-in-idleness* was the folk name for the wild pansy or
       heartsease often used in love potions)

Night Thought

Fingers on black silk
defy the night's dark shadows
with gifts of desire.

Stolford

March's wish fulfilled
in a caravan for three
naked morning tea

.

Dust

Sunday morning sunlight
slides through lazy curtain traps
spreading its tender hand over my back
– such an unhurried lover.
No reason to stir, no demand
to shake dreams away just yet.

I'll wish deep, inappropriately,
scandalously laying
bright yellow daffodils
of want on pale pillows
cooled from sleep.
Wrapped in the duvet's crisp snow,
I will conjure you again.

Your new year gift catches the dust
a naked leg stirs, lazy light
spiralling small diamond thoughts
in to the warming air, dead souls
transformed, delivered as day stars
blinking over an eager white sea –
the way you reach me.

Your hands form the dream
that beckons, that fills
this empty, frosted bed.
As I turn my eyes inward
you are there.

Hand Words

The words that hands speak
are more eloquent than
a thousand specially
chosen for a mouth.

I have watched your fingers,
your hands, your wrists –
have had to handcuff mine.

Swan

I believe you.
Even the small stars
you drew down my back
a constellation,
not a promise blown
away in the slyness
of sudden twisters.
My dark was never
too deep
for your word.
So I keep it,
and learn to love
like a swan.

River Exe mussels with chilli, tomato and parsley

The foreplay is with warm bread and olive oil:
you dripped,
I licked my lips like a cat.
Then the mussels arrive
with just-opened steam
and a light dandruff of parsley.
You drool slightly
before choosing, teasing
the dark, hard lips
to reveal a first soft pearl.
You suck its sweetness
leaving a light aftermath
of garlic.

The Exe has done its work well.

I cross my legs
as you pluck and prick
with your perfect poet's fingers,
slipping them between
teeth and tongue tip
dipping into the oil slick
finger-bowl –
in out, out in, dripping
frivolity, not necessity.

O lucky bowl.
O lucky tongue.

You will spoon the juice slowly
saying the spice is just right
the flavours lingering:
"Just hot enough."
If only he knew.

We refuse dessert.

Over the Table

When you write
you are private
like a clam
who is not a clam at all
but an oyster
quietly turning
a piece of sand
into a pearl.

A Late Bloom

It was a late bloom
blushing as November leant against it.
No woollen shift or cotton stay
but brave in silk and dissolute,
lace-topped.

Wind played fingers
over pleasured petals
like harp strings, rippling
scarlet petticoats
and long lovers' legs
until she dropped
each undergarment on the carpet.

The seed so set
from tiny tell-tale pockets
will be gathered on a lip,
will be made to wear
a vow of silence.

Henna On Her hands

She will wear her lemon chiffon sari
with an ochre blouse and petticoat.
She will walk barefoot,
letting whispers of silk kiss her ankles.
Bells sing in a late sunlight.

She will tread over sandalwood
and jasmine to the old women
to have henna painted on her palms,
on white porcelain feet, as a blessing.
They will fuss her paleness.

In the baked red kitchen clay
they unveil a secrecy, a pattern,
stitching it with paste vines, leaves,
earth flowers until roots stick,
until she breathes the ancient.

They talk with women words
blushing the room in an innocence
whilst she washes in herbs, anoints herself
with oil from a cracked jar,
playing with another's skin.

Bracelets sing on busy wrists
and, happy with her hidden sister, Daxia
gives a small vermillion bindi
for her head, as a seal, a sign, an eye
for the nine day dance.

Then let us take the garba pot
and spin each other's skirts
around a wheel, an earth, finding
that difficult, delicate rhythm.
We hold each other in the round

wearing one another;
none so very different.

Sentence

In this life's sentence
I have been finding commas.
You are my full stop.

Shall I Write

Shall I write that the evening is topaz
though it stutters in blue, is opening
 my window with a crack in its voice.

Shall I say that the cloud, in its late rush,
has sunlight dancing on its far edge
where you helped me to put it, though it is grey.

Shall I pretend that the day has played
music over rooftops to my muffled ears
though its fists have punched me.

Shall I put that I have found a smile
wrapped in tissue at the bottom of a drawer
though I am not sure it is mine.

Shall I say that the miles are not long
and I will unwind an easy route
though my weekend bag is breaking.

Or shall I just write that the world is all rain,
the land hard, the light curved,
and I am alone and wanting you.

Given

To the giver of all things invisible of worth
intertwined in my hands
unlike any other.

To the conjuror, the sorcerer
the finder of paths and desire
in my wasteland.

To the maker of words that pirouette
in morning mist over blue black hills,
to the mouth of an evening dog.

To the owner of ice blue eyes
the last thing I see
the first thing I wait for this morning

I give you today
one heart.

Indigo Dreams Publishing
24, Forest Houses
Cookworthy Moor
Halwill
Beaworthy
Devon
EX21 5UU
www.indigodreams.co.uk